VIOLA

Intermediate Scales AND Bowings

for STRINGS

by HARVEY S. WHISTLER and HERMAN A. HUMMEL

C O N T E N T S

RUBANK®

HAL•LEONARD® CORPORATION
7777 W. BLUEMOUND RD. P.O. BOX 13819 MILWAUKEE, WI 53213

Key of C Major

Détaché Scale

1

Use détaché bowing in (1) LOWER HALF, (2) MIDDLE, and (3) UPPER HALF of bow.

Relative Minor Scales and Chords

Use détaché bowing in (1) LOWER HALF, (2) MIDDLE, and (3) UPPER HALF of bow.

2

3

Scales and Chords in Eighth Notes

Also practice (1) slurring each two notes, and (2) slurring each four notes.

4

5

6

Staccato Scales

Use short strokes in (1) LOWER HALF, and (2) MIDDLE of bow.

7

8

Scale and Chord in 6/8 Meter

Triplets

Use (1) LOWER HALF, (2) MIDDLE, and (3) UPPER HALF of bow.

Dotted Eighth and Sixteenth Notes

Use (1) LOWER HALF, (2) MIDDLE, and (3) UPPER HALF of bow. Also practice at the FROG with a separate bow for each note.

Be sure to start UP BOW. Play at extreme tip of stick, using about four inches of hair.

AT POINT

Articulated Scales and Chords

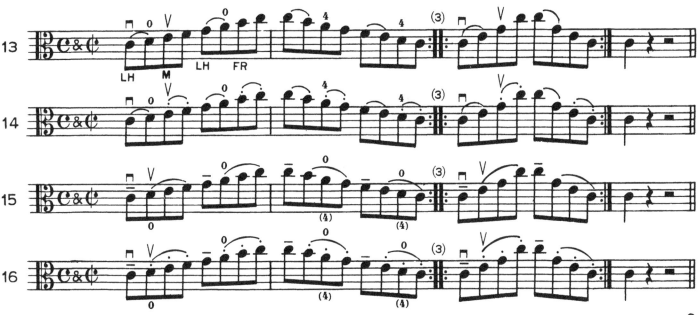

Key of G Major

Détaché Scale

Use détaché bowing in (1) LOWER HALF, (2) MIDDLE, and (3) UPPER HALF of bow.

Relative Minor Scales and Chords

Use détaché bowing in (1) LOWER HALF, (2) MIDDLE, and (3) UPPER HALF of bow.

Scales and Chords in Eighth Notes

Also practice (1) slurring each two notes, and (2) slurring each four notes.

Staccato Scales

Use short strokes in (1) LOWER HALF, and (2) MIDDLE of bow.

Scale and Chord in 6/8 Meter

25

Triplets

Use (1) LOWER HALF, (2) MIDDLE, and (3) UPPER HALF of bow.

26

Dotted Eighth and Sixteenth Notes

Use (1) LOWER HALF, (2) MIDDLE, and (3) UPPER HALF of bow. Also practice at the FROG with a separate bow for each note.

27
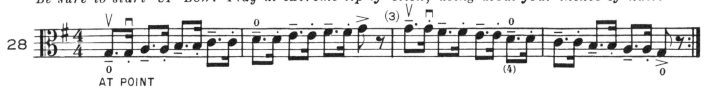

Be sure to start UP BOW. Play at extreme tip of stick, using about four inches of hair.

28

AT POINT

Articulated Scales and Chords

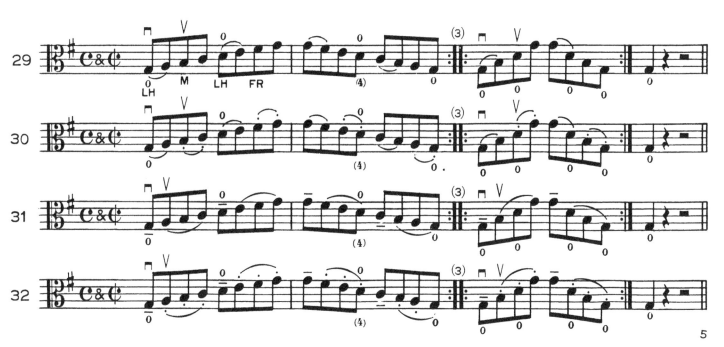

29

30

31

32

5

Key of D Major

Détaché Scale

Use détaché bowing in (1) LOWER HALF, (2) MIDDLE, and (3) UPPER HALF of bow.

Relative Minor Scales and Chords

Use détaché bowing in (1) LOWER HALF, (2) MIDDLE, and (3) UPPER HALF of bow.

Scales and Chords in Eighth Notes

Also practice (1) slurring each two notes, and (2) slurring each four notes.

Staccato Scales

Use short strokes in (1) LOWER HALF, and (2) MIDDLE of bow.

Scale and Chord in 6/8 Meter

41

Triplets

Use (1) LOWER HALF, (2) MIDDLE, and (3) UPPER HALF of bow.

42

Dotted Eighth and Sixteenth Notes

Use (1) LOWER HALF, (2) MIDDLE, and (3) UPPER HALF of bow. Also practice at the FROG with a separate bow for each note.

43

Be sure to start UP BOW. Play at extreme tip of stick, using about four inches of hair.

44

AT POINT

Articulated Scales and Chords

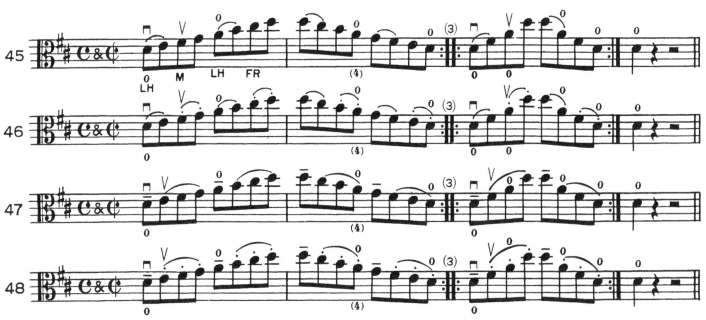

45

46

47

48

Key of A Major

Détaché Scale

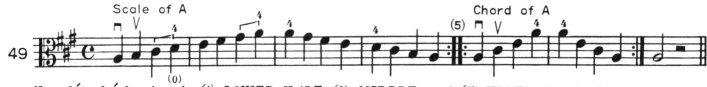

Use détaché bowing in (1) LOWER HALF, (2) MIDDLE, and (3) UPPER HALF of bow.

Relative Minor Scales and Chords

Use détaché bowing in (1) LOWER HALF, (2) MIDDLE, and (3) UPPER HALF of bow.

Scales and Chords in Eighth Notes

Also practice (1) slurring each two notes, and (2) slurring each four notes.

Staccato Scales

Use short strokes in (1) LOWER HALF, and (2) MIDDLE of bow.

Scale and Chord in 6/8 Meter

Triplets

Use (1) LOWER HALF, (2) MIDDLE, and (3) UPPER HALF of bow.

Dotted Eighth and Sixteenth Notes

Use (1) LOWER HALF, (2) MIDDLE, and (3) UPPER HALF of bow. Also practice at the FROG with a separate bow for each note.

Be sure to start UP BOW. Play at extreme tip of stick, using about four inches of hair.

Articulated Scales and Chords

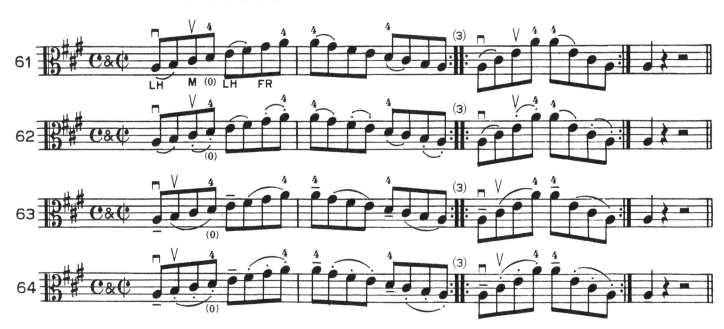

Key of F Major
Détaché Scale

65

Scale of F / Chord of F

Use détaché bowing in (1) LOWER HALF, (2) MIDDLE, and (3) UPPER HALF of bow.

Relative Minor Scales and Chords

Use détaché bowing in (1) LOWER HALF, (2) MIDDLE, and (3) UPPER HALF of bow.

66 D Harmonic Minor / D Minor

67 D Melodic Minor / D Minor

Scales and Chords in Eighth Notes

Also practice (1) slurring each two notes, and (2) slurring each four notes.

68 F Major / F Major

69 D Harmonic Minor / D Minor

70 D Melodic Minor / D Minor

Staccato Scales

Use short strokes in (1) LOWER HALF, and (2) MIDDLE of bow.

71 *simile*

72

Scale and Chord in ⁶⁄₈ Meter

Triplets

Use (1) LOWER HALF, (2) MIDDLE, and (3) UPPER HALF of bow.

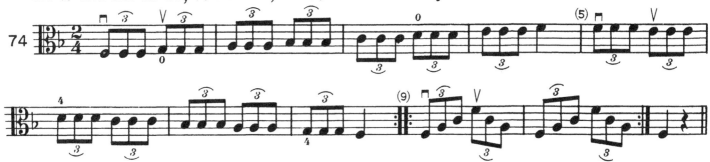

Dotted Eighth and Sixteenth Notes

Use (1) LOWER HALF, (2) MIDDLE, and (3) UPPER HALF of bow. Also practice at the FROG with a separate bow for each note.

Be sure to start UP BOW. Play at extreme tip of stick, using about four inches of hair.

AT POINT

Articulated Scales and Chords

Key of B♭ Major
Détaché Scale

81

Use détaché bowing in (1) LOWER HALF, (2) MIDDLE, and (3) UPPER HALF of bow.

Relative Minor Scales and Chords

Use détaché bowing in (1) LOWER HALF, (2) MIDDLE, and (3) UPPER HALF of bow.

82

83

Scales and Chords in Eighth Notes

Also practice (1) slurring each two notes, and (2) slurring each four notes.

84

85

86

Staccato Scales

Use short strokes in (1) LOWER HALF, and (2) MIDDLE of bow.

87

88

Scale and Chord in 6/8 Meter

89

Triplets

Use (1) LOWER HALF, (2) MIDDLE, and (3) UPPER HALF of bow.

90

Dotted Eighth and Sixteenth Notes

Use (1) LOWER HALF, (2) MIDDLE, and (3) UPPER HALF of bow. Also practice at the FROG with a separate bow for each note.

91

Be sure to start UP BOW. Play at extreme tip of stick, using about four inches of hair.

92

Articulated Scales and Chords

93
94
95
96
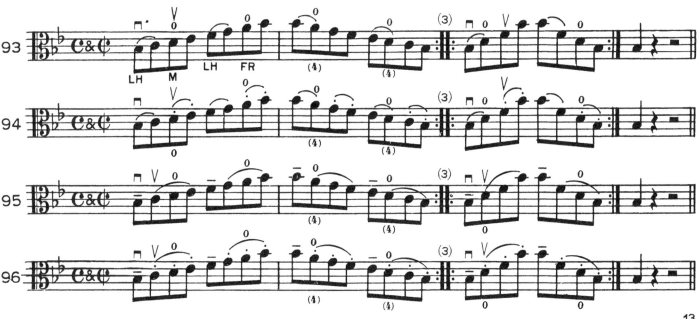

13

Key of E♭ Major

Détaché Scale

97

Use détaché bowing in (1) LOWER HALF, (2) MIDDLE, and (3) UPPER HALF of bow.

Relative Minor Scales and Chords

Use détaché bowing in (1) LOWER HALF, (2) MIDDLE, and (3) UPPER HALF of bow.

93

99

Scales and Chords in Eighth Notes

Also practice (1) slurring each two notes, and (2) slurring each four notes.

100

101

102

Staccato Scales

Use short strokes in (1) LOWER HALF, and (2) MIDDLE of bow.

103

104

14

Scale and Chord in 6/8 Meter

105

Triplets

Use (1) LOWER HALF, (2) MIDDLE, and (3) UPPER HALF of bow.

106

Dotted Eighth and Sixteenth Notes

Use (1) LOWER HALF, (2) MIDDLE, and (3) UPPER HALF of bow. Also practice at the FROG with a separate bow for each note.

107

Be sure to start UP BOW. Play at extreme tip of stick, using about four inches of hair.

108

AT POINT

Articulated Scales and Chords

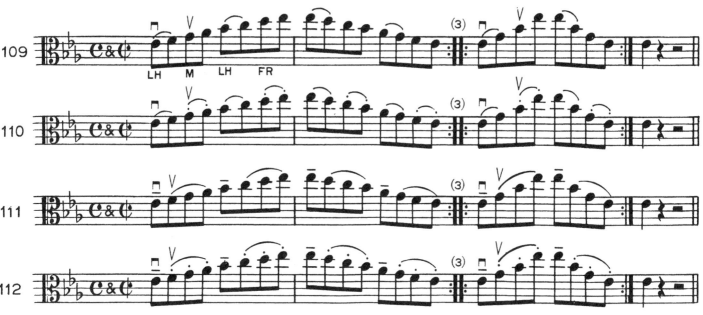

109

LH   M   LH   FR

110

111

112

Chromatic Scales

FIRST POSITION FINGERING

Ascending from open string: 0- 1- 1- 2- 2- 3- 4
Descending from fourth finger: 4- 3- 2- 2- 1- 1- 0

Also practice (1) slurring each two notes, and (2) slurring each four notes.

Extended Chromatic Scale